BEFORE

YOU TRADE

A beginner's guide to avoid losing money while trading.

SAVANIA CHINA

Simple strategies that will save you thousands

Truths that your broker and the big banks do not want you to know

Learn how the system is 'rigged' and how you can also 'play the game.'

SAVANIA CHINA

Introduction

Why you may want to listen to my advice about trading?

First and foremost, I must come out and state that I do not have and am not promising, a secret formula or strategy to beat the market. If you are looking for that, well, don't. Because such a magic formula does not exist. If it did, whoever had it would have scooped up all the profits and wiped the markets clean. The only reason the market works, and has worked for hundreds of years, is because there is no magic formula to beat it. Even the people on the inside do not possess any "insider magic wands".

But what I lack in magic formulas I make up in experience. And by 'experience' I am not referring only to time, in other words the number of years spent trading. Experience can also be measured in the variety, frequency, and ferocity of the hits we take in life, events that shape and define our lived experience. In my short time as a trader, I experienced the highs and the lows of trading. I made tons of money, but lost just as much, if not more.

I thought I was the "Wolf of Wall Street" type - a slick, smooth guy who had it all figured out. Having done all the fancy stuff like attending a top business school, studying for an MBA, and holding a senior position in Westminster, I fooled myself into believeing I was as smart and capable as anyone and would therefore easily play and beat the market. But boy was I wrong.

After a few weeks of making huge gains on the market, mostly through spread betting, it all came crashing down one December morning in 2015. I had betted huge on the Spanish market pending the results of an election. The election results were unexpected, and the market plunged. A few panicked decisions later, I lost everything, every penny I had in my name.

So, I am indeed that guy, the guy who got crushed and humbled by the markets and learned some serious lessons along the way.

While I could never claim to be an outstanding trader, I do know a thing or two about making and losing money on the stock market.

Especially losing money

So, why should you listen to me? It's simple. Imagine you have a container that you want to fill with water. Besides actually pouring water into the container, what should you check for first? Yes, you are right, you must check for holes. I'm sure you agree with me that the only way you can ever fill the container is by making sure there are no holes at the bottom through which water can escape. If there are holes at the bottom, that bucket will never fill up no matter how much water you pour into it. The same is true with trading. No matter how much money you make, you will never get rich if you don't know how not to lose money. It's as simple as that. And that is where I and this little guidebook come in.

A few clarifications

What this guidebook is

A short (30 - 60 minute) guide on things you should consider and know as a trader to avoid losing your money on the stock market.

What it's not

This book is not an instructional manual on how to trade or how to invest on the stock market.

What type of trading is covered?

This guide covers online trading: spread-betting, contracts for difference (CFDs), Forex, Shares and Exchange Traded Products.

The Basics

Trading is simple. It is like any other business - you buy something cheap and sell it at a higher price. The difference between the two prices (minus expenses) is your profit. Same applies to trading on the market - whether you are buying shares or spread betting. I am not going to go into great detail about the different types of things you can trade in this guide. However, I will touch on a few instruments towards the end. But the basic concept is that you buy something at a low price and sell at a higher price. With spread-betting and other things like futures, it doesn't necessarily have to happen in that order. In other words, you can sell something first when the price is high and buy it back when it's lower.

Before you start trading – peruse and choose.

Even if you are already trading, this is important

Most people who are new to online trading want to try it all - foreign currency, spread-betting, shares, futures, exchange traded products, etc. Here is a piece of advice. Don't do that! This is what you should do instead. Before you start, read around and compare and contrast. There is a lot of free and paid-for material to help you. Then choose one. Yes, at the beginning choose one or two (but no more than two, and I cannot emphasise this enough!) things to trade you think will suit you best. In this guide, I provide an overview on shares, exchange-traded products (ETPs), forex, and spread betting. My emphasis is not on how these products work but how not to lose money when trading them. In other words, I will show you how to minimise losses when trading any of these products.

Once you have chosen what you want to

trade, go back to read and find out more about your choice. Most brokers and spread betting firms will provide some tutorials and guides.

Useful resources can be found on websites like www.fool.co.uk, www.stockopedia.com, etc. There are plenty of sites that explain the differ-ent (instruments)things you can trade and how they work. Make sure you read more than one to get a balanced view.

Don't make this mistake!   Most of us make the mistake of spending a lot of time researching ways to beat the market or researching loop-holes/unique methods or pieces of information that will give us an advantage over everyone else. It is an understandable human weakness that we are drawn to seek such an advantage. That was the mentality I had when I started trad-ing. But doing so is not only misguided, it sets us on the wrong path. My advice is that you should put in the work to learn how it all works - properly. No cheating or shortcuts here.

Put in the effort to truly understand the mechan-ics of it all. It sounds boring, but it is important.

Just think back to your school days - who ended up doing well - the boy/girl who found a way to cheat the tests or the one who really understood how things worked? Don't be tempted to obsess over finding out the secret to big profits. Knowing the fundamentals will save you a lot of money, if not make you a lot of money. Remember it is much easier to cheat a system you know well than one you don't.

Now choose a broker or spread betting firm.

Your success depends on making a good choice.

Numerous online sources compare brokers and firms that provide trading services in different countries. It is important that you choose an appropriately registered and regulated broker. I could not emphasise this more.

Choosing a registered and regulated broker or firm will mean you get your money back if something goes wrong with the broker (for example, due to bankruptcy, closure, etc.)

In the UK, all regulated firms are covered by the Financial Services Compensation Scheme, which guarantees traders a compensation of up to £50 000 if a broker goes bust. The regulations are different in other countries. Make sure you understand the regulatory and legal protections in your country or state.

For UK investors, I have put together a table of reputable online trading firms and brokers. I believe the majority of these platforms also cater for non-UK traders.

Broker	Shares/ Exchange Traded Products	Futures/ Options	Spread betting	Contracts for Difference	Foreign Currency
barclaysstock-brokers.co.uk	√	X	√	√	X
capital-spreads.com	X	X	V	√	√
cityindex.co.uk	X	X	√	√	√
cmcmar-kets.co.uk	X	X	√	√	√
etxcaptial.co.uk	X	X	√	√	√
fxcm.com	√	√	√	√	√
fxpro.co.uk	X	X	X	√	√
hl.co.uk	√	X	√	√	√
idealing.com	√	√	√	√	√
ig.com	√	X	√	√	√
interac-tivebrokers.co.uk	√	√	X	√	√
iii.co.uk	√	X	√	√	√
iweb-sharedeal-ing.co.uk	√	X	X	X	X
oanda.co.uk	X	X	X	√	√
plus500.co.uk	X	X	X	√	√
uk.saxomar-kets.com	√	√	√	√	√
selftrade.co.uk	√	X	X	X	X
share.com	√	X	X	X	X
spreadco.com	X	X	√	√	√
tddirectinvest-ing.co.uk	√	√	√	√	√

Notable UK online trading platforms, 2017
Please note this is historical and may have since changed.

Choosing the right broker is crucial. But how do you know or choose a good one? It all comes down to your intentions. My advice is that you should be aware and watch out for the following.

- **Costs.** Keep them low. Brokers are in the business to make money. They do so by charging you to execute your trades. They do this through commissions, dealing fees and other charges. Even if a broker offers low fees be aware of less obvious or <u>hidden charges</u>. Another thing worth noting here is that while spread-betting does not incur a fee as such, it is still **not free.** The charges are built into the spreads. So, the bigger the spread, the more expensive.

- If you want to trade shares, some firms charge very high commission for shares that are priced in foreign currency.

- Make sure your broker is properly registered and regulated. In the UK, they should be registered and regulated by the FSCS.

- Make sure the broker's trading platform is reliable - go to online forums to see if there is any negative feedback on the platform's performance. I had one bad experience where I was trying to close out a position that was losing me money and the platforms just froze. I had to re-start my laptop before I could log back on and finally close that trade - and lost a few thousand pounds as a result.

- If you are a short-term and frequent stock trader, you need to be aware of what type of access your broker has to the market. This affects the speed and efficiency at which they put through your orders. There are two types of market access.

  - *Quote Driven System.* With this system, you do not directly buy or sell on the London Stock Exchange, for example. Instead, when you place a trade, your broker will present it to a group of what are known as retail service providers (RSPs). Your broker will then present to you the best quote (price) which you then have limited time (a few seconds) to accept. Remember you are not buying or selling on the actual exchange like the London Stock Exchange, but to and from RSPs

- *Order Driven System or Direct Market Access.* In this case, your trade is placed directly on the stock exchange until someone accepts your price. You can usually get better prices using this system. This system also allows you to order outside trading hours. However, very few providers offer this in the UK. As of January 2017, only the following did - IG, iDealing, Interactive Brokers and Saxo Capital Markets (again, this is historical and may have since changed)

Practice with a Demo Account for months

Most trading platforms will allow you to open a demo account to practice trading with virtual money before you try with real money. This is a great opportunity to learn about the charts, placing orders, using indicators, etc. It's a no-brainer that you <u>must</u> practice with such an account. Most people do, but they don't do it properly or enough.

What do I mean by that? Well, most of us do it for a very short time, say a week or so. And we usually do relatively well on a demo account which gives us a false sense of confidence to switch to the real thing quickly.

There is one simple reason why we do well with demo trading accounts - we don't trade with our emotions. After all, it is not real money. We don't risk losing anything, so we are naturally calmer and reasonable. But as any trader knows - we lose that cool the moment we put our own money on the line. Later in this guide, I will give you a few tips on how to keep your cool (and your hair).

After practising on a demo account for months, you should finally open a real account. When I started, I kept both a demo and a real account. I would practice new strategies on the demo account and only apply them to my real account if they worked. I strongly advise that you adopt this method.

Now that you are actively trading let's focus on what matters more than making money - not losing it.

How not to lose money

or, at least, minimise your losses

Most of us go into trading with the simple objective to make money - lots of it. We are usually driven by the desire to either get rich (quick) or get out of financial trouble. You can't fault anyone for wanting to make money or wanting a better life. But herein lies the problem. We get into trading with only one objective - <u>making money</u>. And we pay less attention to the other side of the equation - <u>losing money</u>. You are probably thinking, wait a minute, doesn't 'wanting to make money' imply that you don't want to lose money? As it turns out, it doesn't. The two things are not the same.

Here is what most of us think will happen when we trade (pic)

Most of us are filled with visions of making heaps of money. I am not going to lie, it's not a bad thing to have high aspirations and a positive mentality, but it needs to be balanced.

However, the reality of trading (or the statistics or data) paints a very different picture. The reality is that more individual traders, **people like you and me** (also known as retail investors) **lose money more than they make it.**

Estimates of the proportion of individual traders who lose money vary between 60% and 80%. You are probably wondering now how that is possible, because you have heard, and seen, so many stories of people who made fortunes through online trading - ordinary people like you and me. Books have been written about people who went from nothing to making billions through trading.

There are living billionaires like Warren Buffet, George Soros, etc. who made their billions on the stock market. So how is it that I am suggesting more people lose money than make money through trading?

The explanation is simple. If I make 1 million on the stock market, I am likely to shout about it, right? What if I lose £1000? I probably won't even tell my spouse/partner, let alone my friends, family, and strangers. The sad reality is that when you lose a few hard-earned thousands (even hundreds), you are just one of the many millions of small retail investors who lose a little at a time, and whose losses become the forgotten statistics that get buried under the few success stories and clever marketing. Your, and my losing a few dollars/pounds (insert currency) is not unique. It's not even a story worth telling, and it rarely ever gets told.

That is why we get the illusion that we are likely to cash in on the markets than we are to lose. Ultimately that leads us, like I mentioned earlier, down a path where we focus mostly on the outcome that we want and believe is likely - **making money!** And ignoring the outcome that, according to data, is more likely to happen - **losing money.**

But you should always remember - the only stories that get the coverage are the rare success stories. That, unfortunately, distorts reality. It makes most of us think that making money on the market is commonplace. One other thing that makes us think that making money on the stock market is the norm is the source of our information.

Besides hearing directly from the fewer than 5% (more like 1%) of traders who were lucky enough to reap huge rewards from trading, we get most of our information and encouragement from institutions that stand to benefit from our trading - **big banks, brokers, and institutional investors**. Don't ever get it twisted, these institutions do not, and I repeat, **they do not care about you.** Their one and only objective is to make money off you. And they can do that whether you make money or not. All they care about is that you trade. So they only provide you with information that will encourage you to trade.

Ok, let's get one thing straight. Money doesn't get 'lost' on the market - it is just transferred or exchanged. So, when 60% - 80% of us lose money on the markets, where do you think it goes? It doesn't fall into an abyss or disappear into nothingness. If I invest or trade £1 000 of real money and lose all of it, it simply goes to someone else. And where do you think it goes? You guessed right - banks, brokers, institutional investors, and the like.

This is a crucial point to remember here, and it's not a conspiracy theory or anything of that nature. It is a fact and reality that is so obvious yet for some unknown reason it does not seem so to most of us.   I will come back to this point later.

What else should convince you that the odds of making money as an individual trader/investor are stacked against you?   The answer is simple - look no further than Wall Street, or the City of London!

For one second consider the number of

extremely smart people who work for the big banks on Wall Street and the City of London. Now, ask yourself this. If it were easier to make lots of money as an individual trader why would these very smart people, who by the way know how the system works a million times better than you and I, continue to toil for these companies? There must be a reason, right? Otherwise, it wouldn't make any sense for bankers to toil long hours when they could be cashing in from just minutes of online trading from the comfort of their living rooms or some beachfront property in the Bahamas.

Believe me, those Wall Street types really know how the system works. I attended business school with some of them and had a chance to work with them closely. They are just as driven, if not more, as you and me. They want to make money, probably more than you and me. They also have a lot more capital to invest and play with than you and me. Yet they don't.

Just stop and ponder that for a moment.

Why are they not walking out of banks, investment companies, and brokers to trade on their own and profit from the market? After all, they have a lot of 'insider' knowledge and experience.

I think I have made my point. Making a lot of money through trading is not easy. This is probably something you didn't want to hear, but it's important that you do.

And it's important to acknowledge that losing money is the likely outcome because it will make you realise the value of learning how not to lose money.

Being aware of these harsh realities will make you realise the value of this little inexpensive publication, because it will help you learn to deal with the most likely outcome of your investment and trading efforts.

Most articles, books, etc. tend to focus on teaching you how to make money; or how to beat the markets. To reiterate an earlier point, you can't really beat the market. If it were possible a lot of smart people would have left Wall

Street to make billions as independent traders.

Don't invest a lot of your time learning tricks to beat the market. The market is like a lottery. No one can teach you how to win a lottery.

Accept that you will lose more times than you win

This is one of the most important things to learn and accept as soon as you decide to become a trader. It doesn't necessarily mean you will lose more money. It means you may lose **more times** than you win. Why is this point critical?
It means you must make sure your losses are small. That is the key to not losing money. **Make your losses small, and your wins big**. That is what big banks and institutions do. The statistics suggest they lose about 60% of the time. But the 40% that they win, they win big.

As an individual trader, you should adopt the same approach. Minimise your losses and max-imise your wins. You can do this by hedging your investments (shares) or using stop/trailing losses (spread betting).

I will give you an example of the strategy that I used for my spread betting account.

	Cost per trade (£)	Number of trades	Total Loss/Gain
Loss (if trade loses)	20	70	-1400
Gain (if trade goes my way)	50	30	1500
			100 (profit)

Based on the above **strategy,** with every trade I made I risked losing £20 with the potential to win £50. I used stop losses to enforce this rule. As you can see from the chart if I made 100 trades a day and lost money on 70 and won on 30, I would still make a profit of £100 on that day (the spread i.e. fees are already accounted for in the winnings or losses).

This is a straightforward strategy to follow. You can change the numbers - maybe increase the size of your bets and reduce the number of trades if you are not a **high-volume** trader and still achieve the same results.

With this **strategy,** it is important to make sure you take money out when you are winning. When I started trading, I made the mistake of wanting more, of being greedy. It's an affliction that affects most new traders. Beware of it.

When I was in a winning trade, I wanted to let it run for as long as possible to maximise my profits. Sometimes that would turn against me, and I would end up closing the position with a loss or a very small gain.

So, it is as **IMPORTANT to take out your wins as it is to stop your losses**.

This strategy also works by taking the emotions out of trading. Most traders almost tear their hair out on every trade because they want to win on every trade. Or they don't want to lose on any trade. That is very stressful and unsustainable because you simply can't win all the time.

When you have a strategy that allows you to lose more than half the time, you will not stress over each and every trade. You don't even need to sit and watch. You simply place an order, and the outcome is either it makes you money or loses a bit. What matters is that at the end of the day your winnings outweigh or are equal to your losses.

Don't trade with your emotions

This is probably not the first or the last time you will hear this. We hear this a lot, yet it's one of those 'easier said than done' type of things. When you are risking a chunk of your kids' college fund, pension, or that 'rainy day money' on a trade, it's difficult to keep your cool.

Most of the losses that traders incur are a result of panicking. We panic due to temporary fluctuations, which in turn force us to act too quickly or irrationally. I will cover this later in the guide, especially in the spread-betting section.

Strategies like the one I outlined above will take the emotions out of your trading. Remember to trade with the mindset of an institution or bank. Imagine if a supermarket obsessed over every bottle of milk or loaf of bread, that would not be sustainable. It would drive them mad. Luckily, they don't. Instead, they are happy as long as they make more money from the bread and milk they sell than the money they lose from what they throw away. You should treat your trading the same.

Don't over-trade

Overzealous trading is another common beginners' affliction. I did it when I started out - trading just because I felt like it or wanted to be busy. If you do that, you end up getting into trades without any real reason except being seen to be doing something. You need to have the discipline to wait. Your trading strategy should have a clear reason for getting in and one for getting out.

Unless these conditions are met, you shouldn't do anything. Wait for opportunities. **The best trader is an opportunistic one**. Even those who made billions, like George Soros, were opportunistic. Wait until you definitely have a reason to enter any trade or if something unusual happens that compels you to take a chance to make a quick profit - like when the Chinese market fell rapidly at the beginning of 2016.

You versus big institutions

When you start trading online, remember one thing, money is never lost. It does not disappear into nothingness. When you lose money, it means someone is taking it. And that someone is the big bank, your broker, or other big institutional investors. This is not a conspiracy theory, far from it. It's just a cold fact. Your broker makes money regardless of how you are performing. They make money when you trade, not when you make money. So, their only interest is that you trade more, not that you make money. No matter what your broker tells you, they are not really interested in you making money.

This is important to remember. Watch out for anything that encourages you to trade more or pay more fees. Depending on what you trade, there are ways to make sure that you are not being screwed over with high charges and fees. I will cover this later in the guide

As I have already stated, every time you

make a trade, there is someone on the other side of the transaction. That 'someone' is usually a big institutional investor or, as they are commonly referred to, the big banks. So, when you sell a stock/future etc. it means someone else is buying it from you. And when you buy, it means someone else is selling it to you. What you should ask yourself is - **why**?

Surely, they are not stupid as to buy something that is not worth its price. Nor would they sell something to you if they knew that they could get a better price from selling to someone else or at a different time.

The message here is: when you are trading, try and put yourself in the shoes of the big institutions. When you hear on the news or other financial publications that a certain stock, for example, has just been declared a 'BUY' that should raise a red flag. It means someone is signalling their intent to sell that stock to people like you and me. **Why**?

So, next time you are about to make a 'buy' or 'sell' decision based on the information you got from the media or analysts, ask yourself a few questions like:

- Isn't this what someone wants me to do?
- What's the majority of individual traders like me likely to do with this information?
- What do the big institutions know that I don't? If they are encouraging me to buy, it means they, or someone else, is selling (or vice versa) - the question is **why**?

To avoid losing money, don't always do what everyone else is being asked to do (in trading jargon, this is referred to as 'being contrarian')

Act as if you were an institutional investor. Ask yourself - if you were working for a big bank what would you be doing when retail traders are either buying or selling in a frenzy?

Whatever answer you give – do that!

All the information you have is historical

Here is a rather obvious fact that most of us either ignore or are oblivious to. Whether it's the news or the price charts, we are always behind. Always. Yet with modern technology and overly dramatic media coverage, we are made to believe that the information we are getting is instant and just-in-time. The reality is that it's not. The media and charts are simply telling you what has already happened.

Big institutions have in their possession massive supercomputers that use smart algorithms to execute trades at speeds that are as fast as a thousandth of a second. Yes, that's right. They are that fast. So, when you are sitting in front of your computer looking at charts and feeling empowered, these algorithms are making decisions and trading a thousand times faster than you. This is not to say you should despair. The markets still react to historical data.

So, knowing that the information that you thought was instant is delayed should help you try to predict what happens next and what you need to do before it happens.

Financial products

*Shares, Currencies, Exchange Traded Products,
Spread bets*

Shares (Equities)

When you buy the shares of a listed company, you are buying a piece of the company (or equity in the company). I won't get into too much detail on what shares are, how to pick them etc. My focus is on how not to lose money when investing in them.

How not to lose money?

In 2015 Canadian drug giant, Valeant Pharmaceuticals lost about 60% of its value. There were accusations, by short-selling firms like Citron Research, of bogus activity to inflate revenue. In all honesty, creative accounting is not new. It's a problem that is as old as accounting itself. Most of us have heard about Enron. In a CNBC.com article entitled "*How to avoid getting crushed by stock fraud*", Bryan Borzykowski, said the following about accounting fraud.

"*If it feels like you've heard this story before, it's because you have...Why does it seem as though the professionals – fund managers and analysts – are caught as off guard about these kinds of allegations as the regular investor?.... fund managers also don't have as much incentive as short sellers to call out a company for fraud. In many cases, a mutual fund manager will see something and just not buy that stock.*"

The statement says it all. It reiterates the point I made earlier - that, as a retail investor/trader, you are always on the outside. The institutional investors are at an advantage.

There are a number of ways and reasons you can lose money on shares. Fraud, or 'creative accounting' is one such common reason. This is more commonplace than you think. And the people on Wall Street or in the City of London have very little incentive to call out companies for dodgy practices. If something dodgy is happening, the short-selling firms will know and will do something about it – short sell the shares.

Here is what you need to do to protect your money against such 'fraud' by listed companies.

- Listen to the naysayers. Watch out for short-sellers. If they start short-selling shares be worried and do some research to make sure you are comfortable with your position.
- Make sure there is no suspicious history on the company's senior management (especially the CEO)
- If the company is making a lot of acquisitions be worried. M&As (mergers and acquisitions) tend

> to hide underlying performance problems for the acquiring firm

- When you read a company report, the bad news is usually buried in the footnotes. Pay close attention to the footnotes.
- If all the above exist and you find something negative or suspicious in the footnotes get rid of those shares fast before you lose a lot of money

There is a lot of advice and many tools out there to help you pick shares. Various calculations and indicators are used to help you decide whether to buy, hold, or sell a share. If you are going to avoid losing money you need to be aware of the following:

- The information you have is usually incomplete. The professionals and institutions know far more than you do.
- There is little incentive for institutional investors to tell you, as a regular

investor/trader, about any irregularities. Do your own research and read the small print

- The advice you get to buy or sell is coming from somewhere. And there is a reason why they want you to take that particular action. Ask why!

- Don't focus too much on the price of shares, even indicators like PER (Price - Earnings Ratio) or other ratios. There is always a reason why a share is cheaper or why the PER is low. When making share decisions, focus more on those other reasons (the fundamentals of the business, so to speak), not just the price.

Currencies (Forex)

Unfortunately, this is not my area of expertise. I have not done a great deal of forex trading so feel free to skip this brief section.

Foreign currency trading is a favourite of many beginners.   It is relatively easy to trade forex because you don't need to learn a great deal about companies or charts. Also, exchange rates usually move in line with macroeconomic conditions - inflation, interest rates, etc. That makes it a little 'easier' to 'predict' currency movements. Moreover, Forex trading provides the opportunity that most of us yearn - to make huge profits quickly. Unfortunately, that potential comes with high risk.

How not to lose money in forex?

Forex markets are not very volatile but they do however swing up and down a lot, mostly in small movements. So to compensate for this, most beginners use leverage offered by many trading platforms. Leverage is betting with borrowed money. The best way to minimise losing a lot of money when trading forex is to limit your leverage. When you are starting out, don't leverage more than 15 times (15:1). You will not make a lot of money with that sort of conservative leveraging, but you won't lose a lot either. Just because some trading platforms offer new traders leverage as high as 500:1 does not mean you should take it.   Remember, these platforms make money when you trade, not when you make money.

All the other advice I have already covered about how to read data and charts also apply to Forex

A simple strategy for making money in forex

My limited experience with forex trading is that the best times to make money is during the times of high liquidity - that is when Asian trading hours overlap with European trading hours or European trading hours with American.

You should also be opportunistic with forex trading. Forex tends to react strongly to announcements about economic data from governments or central banks. Mark these on your calendar and try to make money from market reactions. Still, don't bet with huge leverages especially in such opportunistic scenarios.

Spread-betting

The UK is the world's largest spread-betting market. Spread-betting is essentially gambling, in other words, betting that something - be it the FTSE, shares, forex rates, etc - will either go up or down. Like they do with forex trading, brokers allow traders to use leverage (i.e. borrowed money) to make huge bets. That means you can lose more than you put in. Some platforms, like CityIndex, automatically closes out your losing positions at a certain level of margin. That mechanism means you can never lose more than the total in your account from one trade.

The best way to avoid losing a lot of money is to keep the total amount in your spread betting trading account relatively small. It is tempting, if you have the money, to keep large amounts in your trading account in order to maintain big margins and avoid getting 'closed out' automatically during temporary down swings.

One other reason most traders love spread-betting is that it is tax-free.

It is possible to spread bet on Contracts for Difference (CFDs), but CFDs are subject to tax (capital gains tax).

The other difference between straightforward spread-betting and CFDs is that CFDs can incur trading fees and charges. With straight forward spread-betting, the charges are inbuilt into the spread (the difference between the BUY and SELL price). The smaller (tighter) the spread, the cheaper. Most European and US indices trade on very tight spreads - usually 1 point.

However, spread-betting may appear free, but that is simply a massive ILLUSION (see the example on the next page). You do pay a charge for every trade, it's only that it's not so obvious. If you make large bets or keep them open longer, betting on CFDs may be more cost effective.

Example. *Suppose you are spread-betting the FTSE at £10 per point. If the spread is 1 that means the charge for your trade is £10. If you are betting on Wall Street out of hours, the spread is usually as high as 4. If your trade is £10 per point it means your broker earns £40 (10 x 4) per trade from you.*

How not to lose money when spread-betting?

Hidden charges.

Spread betting is very attractive because it is tax-free and there are no extra trading charges? **WRONG**

Spread-betting charges are incorporated into the spreads. Even tight spreads like FTSE100's one point spreads can quickly add up when traded in high volumes. For example, executing 100 trades, each for £5 per point, in a day will add up to £500/day in charges. That is not cheap at all. But you usually get the illusion that it is FREE. So be mindful not to overtrade!

That gets me straight to my second point; a point I have already made but is worth repeating. Your **broker makes money when you trade, not when you make money**.   In the previous example, regardless of how your hundred trades go, your broker will make £500 from you!

So, the best way to not lose money, or to not overpay your broker in hidden fees, is to **not overtrade.** Yes, the less you trade, the better. Be opportunistic, though. Only trade when there is a huge opportunity and your bet is likely to pay off. If you can make big wins a few times a day or even a few times a week or even months - the better. I know it's hard not to put a trade when you are looking at those charts going up and down. But don't. Only do so if it looks like a good opportunity and there is a good reason why the opportunity exists.

Don't trade with your emotions.

I know I am repeating this, but it's worth repeating. Take emotions out of spread-betting. Most beginners place a trade and then sit and watch it as it goes up (Yay!!) or down (Noooo!!). Don't do that. Don't watch your every trade. Adopt a clear strategy, like the one outlined in this guide-book where you put a stop loss and a limit on every trade.

Watch out for your own biases

In his book, *Influence; The Psychology of Persuasion*, Robert Cialdini discusses an interesting phenomenon. He states that:

"A study done by a pair of Canadian psychologists uncovered something fascinating about people at the racetrack: Just after placing a bet, they are much more confident of their horse's chances of winning than they are immediately before laying down the bet. Of course nothing about the horse's chances actually shifts; it's the same horse, on the same track, in the same field; but in the minds of those bettors, its prospects improve significantly once the ticket is purchased. "

Although it may sound puzzling at first, Cialdini explains that this is a psychological phenomenon called Consistency which sits deep within us all. He explains it as an *'obsessive desire to be (and to appear) consistent with what we have already done.*" We feel very strong internal pressure to behave consistently with an earlier decision.

What does this have to do with spread-betting or trading in general, you may be asking? Well, the answer is - a lot. As a psychology enthusiast, I am aware of the hidden psychological mechanisms that compel us to behave illogically. But, when I started trading I fell into the very same psychological traps. Once I made a trade, I became much more attached and confident in the direction of movement than before I made the trade. If my trade went the opposite direction (i.e. started losing money) I would buy or sell even more, consistent with my earlier decision. And the results were not great.   Look at the following example to see what I mean.

....an example

In December 2015, I placed a bet on the ASX200 (The Australian index) believing it would go up as it had just hit its 3-months low. So, I bought it at £5 per point. To my surprise, it kept going down, and I started losing money. Consistent with my earlier logic, I thought if it was cheaper at a 3-months low when I bought it first, it was even cheaper now, so I bought more. It kept going down, and I bought even more. You see where this is going. In the end, I lost a lot of money.

Most traders would identify with this story. It's a psychological mechanism that is inbuilt in us. But it can lead to massive losses. By following a strategy that treats each trade individually, you avoid falling into this pitfall. Use your stop losses to get out of trades that are losing money instead of pumping more money into a losing position.

Simple winning strategies for spread-betting

The best strategy to win with spread betting is to think like an institutional trader. Follow a plan that requires you to win only 30% of the time. So, out of every 10 trades, you will only need 3 to go your way in order to make money. Look at the example of the strategy I used on my portfolio below.

	Cost per trade (£)	Number of trades	Total Loss/Gain
Loss (if trade loses)	20	7	-140
Gain (if trade goes my way)	50	3	+150
			10

The above strategy works because it takes the psychology and emotions out of your trading. It also minimises your losses.

The second most important strategy is to trade less. Be opportunistic instead. You can still apply the above strategy but only waiting for the best opportunities. Although most of us do, you must never trade for the sake of trading. Remember, every time you trade you make your broker rich, whether or not you make money.

Top Tip

One other trick that I discovered is that indices tend to follow each other. There appears to be a very strong link between Wall Street and Australian market. ASX200 usually open by mimicking the Dow Jones and S&P 500. So, watch closely how the American indices close and the Aussie market usually follow suit when it opens. There is a 2-hour gap between the US markets closing and Australian markets opening. I propose you try observing and following this strategy on a demo account for a few weeks first. It always worked for me so it may work for you too.

European indices tend to follow the USA indices. The USA markets react to what happens in China overnight. If you want to make money just map these synergies when spread-betting different indices.

Key points to remember

- Minimise losses - use stop loss on every trade
- Don't be greedy - take profits by using limits
- Don't trade with your emotions or psychological biases. Have a strategy or system
- Don't overtrade. Be opportunistic. Your brokers want you to trade more because that is how they make money
- Remember indices are all interconnected. The US reacts to (but doesn't necessarily follow) China, Australia usually follows the USA on opening.

Exchange Traded Products (ETPs)

Exchange Traded Products (ETPs) are instruments that track other things like stocks, indices, commodities, etc. What that means is that you are essentially buying those things without actually buying them. A good example is that of ETFs (Exchange Traded Funds) which track the stock market indices like the FTSE 100. Most do this on a one-for-one basis. That means the value of your investment follows that of the FTSE. If FTSE goes up by 5%, your investment goes up by 5% as well.

Another type of ETP is Exchange Traded Commodities (ETCs). With ETCs you can buy (invest in) commodities like precious metals and agricultural products without actually buying the physical products. If you are a beginner, I would suggest you stay away from these because they can be very complex.

ETFs can be good for long-term investors who are looking for low fees and do not want to trade regularly. Over time, indices usually go up. When it comes to ETFs:

- Take out profits periodically when indices are high (because they tend to fluctuate a lot - look at the diagram on the next page)
- Hold your nerves at the downturns. It can be unnerving to watch the fall, but it will bounce back.

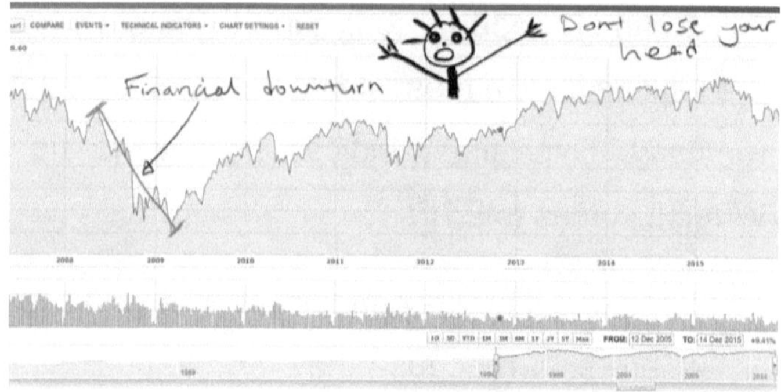

The diagram above shows the 10-year movement of the FTSE100. An ETF tracking the index would have been up 9.4% over that period. As you can see the 2008-2009 downturn saw the index down by 37%.

Anyone who panicked and sold out would have lost a lot of money, but those who held out would have received a decent return.

Leveraged ETPs

Leveraged ETPs do not track indices on one for one basis. Instead, they track indices in multiples. As an example, a x2 leveraged FTSE ETP will rise by 10% if the FTSE rise by 5% in a day.

However, the returns are realised on a **daily basis**. So, if the FTSE goes up 10% a month, it doesn't mean your ETP goes up 20%. You may even lose money. Look at the example below.

The example below is of a x2 leveraged ETP tracking an index over 5 days. Suppose you put in £100 when the index is at 100. A one-for-one ETP will be up 10% on Day 5 (start at £100 and close at £110), but a leveraged ETP will perform as shown in the table below.

Start	100	90	110	120	80
Finish	90	110	120	80	110
Change	-10%	22%	9%	-33%	37.5%
Your ETP	-20%	44%	18%	66%	75%
Your balance	£80	£115	£136	£46	£80
	Day 1	Day 2	Day 3	Day 4	Day 5

Don't worry much about the calculations. The point I'm making is that holding leveraged ETPs over a long time will likely lose you money. In the example, although the index is up 10% on Day 5 (from £100 on day 1 to £110 on Day 5), a leveraged ETP will be down 20% because of the daily fluctuations.

How to not lose money when trading ETPs?

- Stay away from leveraged ETPs at the beginning. It is tempting because the gains can be huge, but so can the losses. However, if you have the heart and stomach for leveraged ETPs, my advice is don't hold them too long. You will likely lose all your money from daily fluctuations.

- Be mindful to keep your costs low. Ask your broker for their Total Expense Ratio (TER). Less than 0.14% is good and anything more than that, not so good.

- Trade ETPs that track the index, commodity, or stock closely. The best way to know how close is to compare the TER and the difference between the ETF and the index. These two should be very closely aligned.

- Trade ETPs with small spreads - that means a small difference between the price you can buy and the price you can sell.

  The smaller the difference, the better.

The best strategies for success with ETPs

I'm not talking about the risky leveraged type of ETPs here. Instead, I am referring to the good old ETFs that most investors buy and hold. The returns are decent, not mind-blowing.

- The best thing is not to lose your head. Don't be unnerved by sharp declines and fluctuations.

- Periodically cash in profits when there is a rise. You stand to make more money by taking out money at the highs. Don't be too greedy and only want to take out money at the highest point though. You don't know where that point is and, frankly, nobody else does. So, set some targets like 10%, 15% or 20% and take profits at such intervals. Set the values at whatever suits you but make sure it is systemic and not something you do on a whim.

Final Remarks

I hope this short guide has covered some useful ground and provided useful tips. The most significant takeaways can be summarised as follows.

- Accept that you will lose more times than you win, but just don't lose more money than you win. Adopt a strategy that allows you to make few big wins and a lot of small losses.
- Don't trade with your emotions and beware of your psychological biases. Adopt a strategy that uses stop losses and limits on every trade.
- Don't overtrade! Wait for opportunities! Brokers make money when you trade, not when you make money. So be wary of any 'suggestions' to trade more.
- It's you versus the big institutions; think and act like them.

- All the information you have is historical, even a 1-minute chart. Every time you see something, remember this - it has already happened. Now try to figure out the next logical step. That's how you will stay ahead.

- **Think costs first!** Everything you do will cost you. Every trade and every transaction cost money! Minimise your total long-term costs - reduce fees, charges, and spreads.

- Markets are all interconnected. Take advantage of these connections to make big profits especially in forex and spread-betting.

About the Author

I am a UK-based trader and author with extensive experience working in London. I studied for an MBA at Warwick Business School, had a great job, but gave up that job to start trading in 2016. That first year, I lost all my money on one bad trade. Even if I had not lost my money on that single trade, I could and perhaps would have lost it eventually because I had never learned the valuable lesson of how not to lose money while trading. I wrote this book to help you avoid the same mistakes I made.

THANK YOU

I hope you enjoyed and found this little guide-book useful.
I would like to thank all my friends and family for their support and unconditional love. I would also like to especially thank my advisor for helping me find my ground when I started trading. Without your support and regular chats on the phone, my losses would've been catastrophic right from the get-go.

✓ Want to receive personal advice and guidance from the author?

✓ Want to read our full catalogue of published books and publications?

✓ Get in touch to ask questions and follow up on any topic?

www.haiems.co.uk

HAIEMS Publishing
United Kingdom

www.ingramcontent.com/pod-product-compliance
Lightning Source LLC
Chambersburg PA
CBHW022118050726
47591CB00002B/837